Pasado

Pasado

The Heart of a Donkey

written by Rebecca Pierce Murray
illustrations by Lori Burkheimer

Bywater Press
Bellingham, Washington

text ©2021 by Rebecca Pierce Murray
illustrations ©2021 by Lori Burkheimer

Published by Bywater Press, Bellingham,Washington
www.bywaterpress.com

First edition, first printing   C D E F G H I K
ISBN: 978-1-7330675-6-0

special dedication

For Timmy

I met you shortly after you left this world. An old soul
in a child's body lying in a casket. I learned you were a
kindred spirit. A lover of animal-kind. Your time here
was cut short. You were only nine when the smoke took
you. My only comfort is knowing you left with your
faithful companion Bella at your side. I know you are
surrounded by animals and people who love you. You
are safe. You are happy. And you are deeply missed.

Timmothy Aaron Barela
March 21, 2011 – September 29, 2020

preface

In April of 2002, I attended a gathering at Pasado's Safe Haven Animal Sanctuary to commemorate the 10th anniversary of Pasado's horrific and senseless death. Standing there, with scores of others, we listened as Susan Michaels, the sanctuary's founder, reminded us of our purpose: to revisit what happened the night of April 15, 1992, when three young men murdered the beloved donkey, Pasado, and then to celebrate the accomplishments of compassionate and motivated people who effected change in his name.

These changes were twofold. The first came in 1994 with a new law named after Pasado to hold those who neglect and harm animals accountable. The second came three years later when Pasado's Safe Haven Animal Sanctuary was founded.

I was inspired to write this book to honor those who strive for better on behalf of animal-kind. It is to remember those who rose from the ashes of grief and despair to make a difference that is now the legacy of a beloved soul named Pasado.

Hee Haw! What am I? I can not hear you! Yes! A donkey! Not to be confused with my cousin the horse. Who would no doubt tell you I am the black sheep of the equine family. But I am no sheep. I am bold. I am crafty. I am Pasado! In Spanish, Pasado means past. Why don't I tell you about mine?

I was born in 1970. An only child, as most donkeys are!

I loved mi mama. She taught me about 'lavida'...life. About how to be with other beings. She said, "Pasado, learn to see the light in the eyes, feel love in the heart, and the fly on the face." SWAT! Sometimes I wish my tail was longer.

Mi mama, she taught me to be gentle with the little ones.

She also taught me 'paciencia'... patience. SWAT! I still have no patience for flies!

My days were so busy: playing, eating, sleeping, dreaming. One day mi mama said to me, "Pasado, my beautiful boy, you are big now! It's time for you to have a place of your own."

Ok, Mama. Good-bye. I will miss you!

I lived in a park in Bellevue, Washington. A place called Kelsey Creek. I had my own pasture, a barn, and a white fence. It was four feet tall all around. There was a beautiful tree in the pasture to give me shade in the summer and an umbrella when it rained. It rains a lot in Bellevue, Washington. Hee-haw!

Every day children came to my fence to pet my nose, scratch my face and wrap their skinny arms around my neck. I would look into their eyes and listen with my big ears as they told me their stories.

I saw light in their eyes.

I felt love in their hearts.

And my heart? Oh! A donkey's heart is pure love.

People, they called me 'beloved'—their beloved Pasado.

They also called me 'vivo'... or, crafty! Perhaps because of the time I found a switch in my barn late at night. I flicked it up and down with my lips. It was fun watching the lights turn on and off again and again.

Later, after the police arrived, they said they thought someone had broken in. They laughed, "Pasado, are you up to your mischief again?" The next morning my guardians put tape on my new toy. They laughed too. "Pasado, you are a crafty donkey!"

I had a good life. I felt happy, safe, and loved. It was all I knew.

Then came the night my life changed. I was sleeping in my barn when I awoke to a noise in my pasture. I poked my head out to see. It was three boys! They were climbing my fence to see me!

I ran to them. But when I got close, I stopped because I saw no light in their eyes.

One of them carried a big rope. He tried to throw it over my neck. I said "No!" and ran back to my barn. I pressed myself against the wall. No! No! No!

They came after me and put the rope around me. Those three boys pulled me out. I fought against them. So hard. I was so afraid.

One boy tied one end of the rope to my beautiful tree.

I tried to run away. But as I ran, the rope got shorter and shorter.

It wrapped around the tree until I couldn't move.

In the morning, my guardians found me laying still against that tree. Skull crushed. Neck crushed. Heart broken.

People were outraged. Who would hurt our Pasado? Who would kill our beloved?

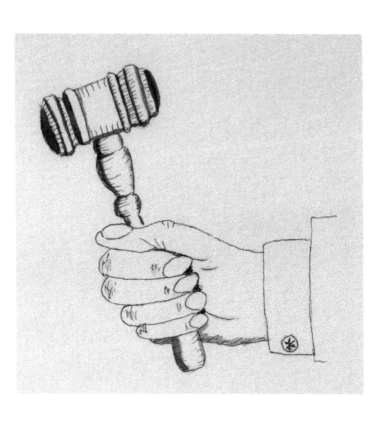

At the trial, the boys confessed to taking my life. They said they beat me with an iron rod because they were mad that I would not let them ride me.

But according to the law, what they did to me was no big deal. Because I was not a 'being.' I was 'property,' 'goods,' a 'thing.'

Again, people were outraged. Many rose up in my name! And thanks to their efforts, two years later, a new law passed to help protect animals. They called it 'The Pasado Law.'

Have you heard of it? No? Have you heard of Google? Yes? Good! You can look it up!

The Pasado Law recognizes animals as beings. Not things. And there would be serious consequences for hurting us.

Also, in my name, Pasado's Safe Haven Animal Sanctuary was founded. It has saved the lives of thousands of animal beings and provided a safe place for many to live out their days in peace and happiness.

Speaking of the sanctuary, would you like to meet some of my sanctuary friends? Oh good! They would like to share their stories with you too!

PASADO'S SAFE HAVEN

Sweet creatures
who pass this way
once scared and alone...
Now you are safe
now you are home.

Here's my friend Splash the Pig. Splash is a funny name for a pig. She will explain.

Hi! My name is Splash! I love my name. My people at the sanctuary gave it to me after I swam across a river to escape my fate as bacon. Yes! That's right! Pigs can swim! Some people are surprised by that. And then, when I tell them I weigh 800 pounds, they say WOWweeee! After crossing that river, I wandered into a lady's backyard. She called her friends at Pasado's sanctuary. When they came to meet me, everyone kept talking about my superior swimming skills! That's when they named me 'Splash.'

I lived at the sanctuary for ten years before I ended up here with Pasado in Animal Heaven. Heaven reminds me a lot of my life at the sanctuary. I have mud puddles to roll in, juicy melons to gobble up, and best of all, there are lots of friendly people here. I especially enjoy my new friend Timmy and his dog Bella who came here together. I love it when Timmy lays against me. He says, "Splash, you're the biggest pillow ever!" That always makes me laugh. I have learned what love is. Love is feeling safe.

Next, I'd like you to meet Tee the Dog!

Hi! My name is Tee! For the first ten years of my life, I lived in someone's front yard chained to a tree. I never went on a walk. I never played. It was not a good life. But it was all I knew. Then one day, someone unchained me from that tree and put me in a car. I'll never forget what it felt like to move like that. It was EXHILLLLLERATING! On that special day, I felt people touch me in a way I'd never felt before. It felt good!

When they brought me here to the sanctuary, the doctors told me I was blind. I was given a big kennel with lots of soft things all around the edges to keep me safe. It makes me happy that I can explore without hurting myself. But the best part of every day is when a nice lady comes to visit me. She helps me do my most favorite thing! I have learned what love is. Love is a car ride!

And finally, here is my friend Harvee, the chicken, to share her story with you.

My name is Harvee. I spent most of my life in a cage with lots of other chickens. There were so many of us we could hardly move! Imagine never being able to walk around and spread your wings! The cages stacked high and long and filled an entire warehouse! Can you imagine the noise and the smell? PEEE EUEEE! It was not a good life. But it was all I knew.

One day I was taken from that place to some-where... BEEEEAUTIFUL. Before that day, I had never been outside. I only knew the feeling of wire mesh under my feet. But for the first time, I felt something soft and green. Can you guess what it was? Yes! It was grass! I was so happy I ran and clucked and spread my wings! YIPPEEEEE! I have learned what love is. Love is grass and grubs and freedom.

Hee Haw! I am happy you got to meet some of my wonderful sanctuary friends. They have taught me much about kindness and compassion. I have also learned a lot from my own story. Yes, it is very sad what happened to me. It still makes many people very angry. But from my death, many good things have come.

A law to punish people who hurt animals? That is good.

An animal sanctuary named after me? That is also good. VERY good! HEE HAW!

But there is one thing I still must say... one thing I know deep down in my donkey soul.

A law would not have prevented my death.
A law cannot prevent cruelty.
A law cannot create compassion.
Only one thing can do that: Love.
Love as pure as a donkey's heart.
Love that would not kill a fly.

SWAT!
Ok, well, maybe a fly.

The ENDS

discussion questions

How does the story of Pasado the donkey makes you feel?

How do you feel when someone is being mean to you?

How do you think an animal feels if someone was being mean to them?

What does the word compassion mean to you?

What are some ways that you can act with compassion for others?

What would you do if you saw a friend hurting an animal?

What are some ways that you can help animals?

Do you believe it is important to speak up when you see someone hurting another person or an animal?

Do you believe that animals have feelings like people do?

Do you believe that animals such as chickens, pigs, and cows have the same feelings as animals like cats and dogs?

How can we show respect to other people, animals, and nature?

afterword

Just one year after Pasado the donkey celebrated his 21st birthday, complete with cake, balloons, and 100 adoring fans in attendance, his life came to an abrupt end. It was the night of April 15th, 1992, that three young men hopped Pasado's 4-foot fence at Kelsey Creek Park, in Bellevue, Washington, carrying a rope tied into a hangman's noose. The following morning a park worker found Pasado dead, with the noose around his neck at the base of his favorite tree. Cuts and bruises covered his body; his skull was crushed, and the rope around his neck had cut a one-inch groove into his flesh.

Within days, a 20-year-old man and two teens were arrested and arraigned. By October, the trial had concluded. The three young men were given minimal sentencing, ranging from 9 months in jail for the then 21-year-old to a mere month, plus community service, for the younger two aged 16 and 18. The three were charged with misdemeanor burglary, which offered a significantly stiffer sentence than the animal cruelty laws would then allow (a maximum of 90 days in jail and a $1,000.00 fine).

The crime and treatment of its perpetrators brought Washington's outdated 1901 animal cruelty law into focus. And Pasado's tragic death provided the momentum for change to finally be made. On June 9, 1994, the efforts of concerned citizens, animal activists, advocates, and lawmakers resulted a new law, known as The Pasado Law. It makes animal cruelty in the first degree a class C felony, imposing a maximum sentence of five years or a fine of up to $10,000, or both.

In 1997, a former Seattle TV personality, Susan Michaels, who had lobbied for The Pasado Law, founded Pasado's Safe Haven Animal Sanctuary, which eventually became an 80-acre farm in Sultan, Washington. The sanctuary provides care for a wide variety of farm and domestic animals. In 2000, Michaels was featured on the Oprah show, which helped expand the sanctuary's audience worldwide. Since Michaels' retirement in 2010, the sanctuary carries forward its mission to rescue and care for animals in need, assist in the prosecution of those who have harmed animals, and educate people around the world in ways to care for animal-kind with compassion, love, and respect.

The photos of Pasado, his mother, and Splash, Tee, and Harvee on the following pages are courtesy of Pasado's Safe Haven.

Visit online at www.pasadosafehaven.org.

about the artist

Lori Burkheimer

Lori's compassion for animals began in her youth with dogs, cats, and two 'camp horses' Nickers and Chippawhah. Today Lori shares her love of animals and nature by creating whimsical miniature watercolor imagery she posts primarily on Instagram @lorib_art and Facebook. Lori resides in Leander, Texas, with her husband, mother, and two adorable rescue Chiweenies, Ziggy and Ralphie.

about the author

Rebecca P. Murray

Rebecca's childhood included many traditional and non-traditional family 'pets' ranging from dogs and cats to exotic snakes, turtles, mice, chicks, various lizards, and even a tarantula.

But it wasn't until she lost her beloved Golden Retriever, Murphy, to cancer in 2000 that her mission to help animals became clear. In her search to invite a new canine into her home, Rebecca became acquainted with the ongoing challenges of her local animal shelter.

The Everett Animal Shelter was woefully under-funded in its attempt to serve the needs of an entire county. As a result, Rebecca felt led to coordinate efforts with shelter staff, city officials, and concerned citizens to establish the shelter's first successful and longstanding volunteer program.

During these early years of the Everett Animal Shelter Volunteer Program, Rebecca met Susan Michaels and became an ardent supporter of the Pasado's Safe Haven Animal Sanctuary.

In 2017, the 25th anniversary of Pasado's murder, Rebecca was moved to write *The Heart of a Donkey* to tell Pasado's story in the first person as a stage presentation. However, she never shared the story because telling it aloud was simply too painful. Then in late 2020, following the publication of her first book, *The Bird and The Hippo*, a friend encouraged Rebecca to push through her pain and publish Pasado's story as a children's book.

Rebecca resides on 20-Acres of wildlife habitat in Mount Vernon, Washington. She lives an idyllic life with her husband, Steve, and two dogs, Martin and Goldie.

Rebecca can be reached through her website at www.rebeccapmurray.com.

In Gratitude

I extend a special thanks to Barbara Gilday for encouraging me to push through the sorrow of Pasado's story and share it with the world.

colophon

This book was designed by Jeffrey Copeland at Bywater Press during the summer and fall of 2021. The text is set in Stone Informal with Stone Sans as a display type. The book was set using the TEX typesetting system and other open source and custom software tools.

The Stone family of fonts were designed by Sumner Stone and Bob Ishi for International Type Corporation, and first released in 1987. TEX was developed by mathematician and computer scientist Donald Knuth. It was originally released in 1978.

Ms Burkheimer's artwork in this volume and on its cover were photographed by Ms Murray.

www.bywaterpress.com

CPSIA information can be obtained
at www.ICGtesting.com
Printed in the USA
LVHW070751130522
718695LV00009B/183

9 781733 067560